Dad's

Get

Rich

Basics

Copyright © 2018 by Joseph L Scicluna
Artwork created by Candace N Scicluna
information@scicluna.com.au

All rights reserved. This book or any portion thereof may not be
reproduced or used in any manner whatsoever without the
express written permission of the publisher except for
the use of brief quotations in a book review.

INTRODUCTION

Hi Kids,

I love being 54. I have so many wonderful memories which bring me joy and happiness. Thank You.

I want to share with you some lessons learned from people wiser than me.

My book of Get Rich Basics will set you on a path of understanding and having money for what you want in life.

It's not a "what to invest in" book.

It's a "what to do" book.

Table of Contents

INTRODUCTION	**4**
DEFINITION OF BEING RICH	**10**
DEFINITION OF BASICS	**14**
THE BASIC RULES	**18**
SPEND LESS THAN YOU EARN	22
SAVE	26
DONATE	30
DO NOT BORROW MONEY UNLESS ASSETS WILL INCREASE IN VALUE	34
SAVINGS ACCOUNTS	**38**
INVESTMENT ACCOUNT	42
EMERGENCY ACCOUNT	46
GOALS ACCOUNT	50
FIND MONEY TO SAVE	**54**
TO BE RICH	**58**
PUT INTO ACTION	**62**

DEFINITION OF BEING RICH

You are rich when you have enough money to pay for your expenses, enough money for the things you want with some to spare, and money put aside for emergencies.

DEFINITION OF BASICS

A set of rules that are the essential part of a system to becoming rich.

THE BASIC RULES

Spend Less Than You Earn

Save

Donate

DO NOT borrow money
Unless assets will increase in value

SPEND LESS THAN YOU EARN

When you receive money, decide how much to save (I suggest at least 10%) and live on the rest. Make sure you do not spend more than you have.

Simple right!

This means you cannot buy anything using credit cards, interest free or buy now pay later.

Only buy things you can afford, using cash or money in your bank account through debit cards etc.

You may need to delay buying some things for a while!

Divide the money you are saving into three separate accounts:

- Investment Account
  - never withdraw - receive returns
- Emergency Account
  - put money aside for the unexpected
- Goals Account
  - save for what you want, then spend and enjoy

Every time you receive money you MUST put some into each of these accounts.

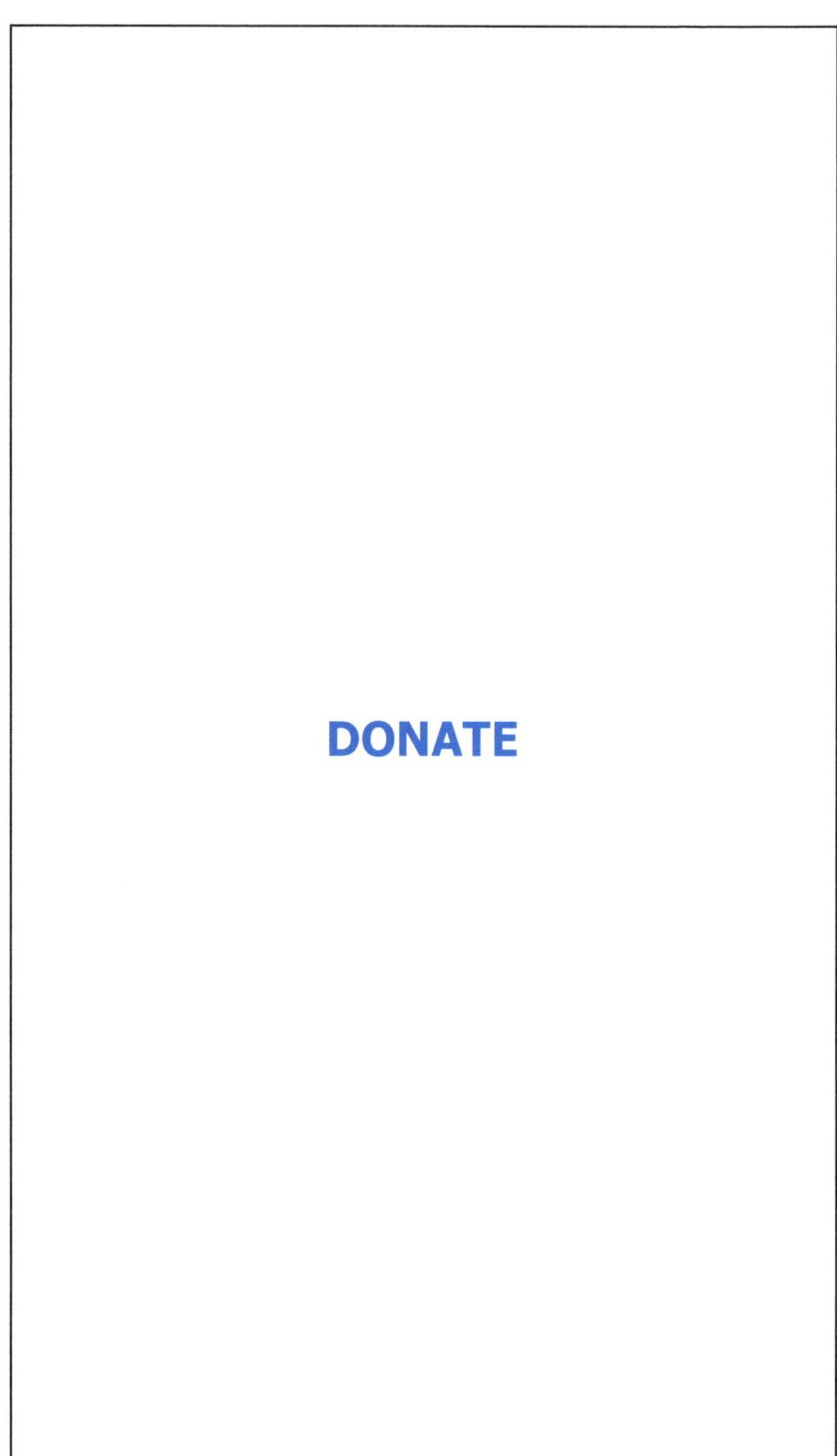

When you receive money, look around, there are always others in a worse situation than you are! So count your blessings and help others. It's a nice thing to do and will help you become Rich.

I know it does not make accounting sense however IT WORKS!

DO NOT BORROW MONEY

UNLESS ASSETS WILL INCREASE IN VALUE

Debt will give the illusion of being rich because it allows you to have THINGS which cost <u>money you do not have</u>.

You and other people may think you are rich, however the day will come when the THINGS have to be paid for.

Everything costs more when you borrow money.

Debit interest never sleeps, gets sick, takes holidays or slows down.

If you do not make your payments you will lose much more than you borrowed.

SAVINGS ACCOUNTS

Investment Account

Emergency Account

Goals Account

The objective of this account is to save enough money to start investing and to use the returns on your investments as your income.

Most of us think we can invest better than someone who has years of study and experience. Usually we are wrong. Let financial advisors do the work for you here.

Or spend the time it takes to learn about investing.

The truly Rich do not work for money.

Money works for them!

EMERGENCY ACCOUNT

The objective of this account is to have money set aside for emergencies that life brings.

Things go wrong, that is part of life, whether it is sickness, a flat tyre, or something breaks; it is good to have some money set aside to pay for them.

The truly Rich are not stressed when things go wrong because they have money to cover it!

GOALS ACCOUNT

The objective of this account is to save for the things you want.

Do not borrow money.

Save your money, then enjoy spending.

The truly Rich spend their own money!

FIND MONEY TO SAVE

Every week most of us throw money away.

By this I mean; when we spend money on things that do not sustain life. Example, chocolates, drinks, fast food, excessive clothing, trinkets, etc.

Not always a bad thing, however once money is spent, it will not come back.

Next time you are about to buy that ??? (chocolate for example) think "do I really need it". If you can do without, send the money to your Investment Account instead, you were going to spend it anyway.

This will grow your investments!

TO BE RICH

In a nutshell, my advice!

- Spend less than you earn
- Save money into three separate accounts (do not mix up the usage), Investment, Emergency & Goals
- Donate
- DO NOT borrow money
  Unless assets will increase in value

You will be rich if you follow these basics because you will have enough money to pay for your expenses, enough money for the things you want with some to spare, and money put aside for emergencies

Love Dad

PUT INTO ACTION

1. Open three bank accounts
    - a. Investment Account
    - b. Emergency Account
    - c. Goals Account
2. Spend less than you earn
3. Put extra money into above accounts
4. Donate some.
5. DO NOT borrow money
   Unless assets will increase in value.

www.ingramcontent.com/pod-product-compliance
Lightning Source LLC
Chambersburg PA
CBHW040234220526
45473CB00001B/244